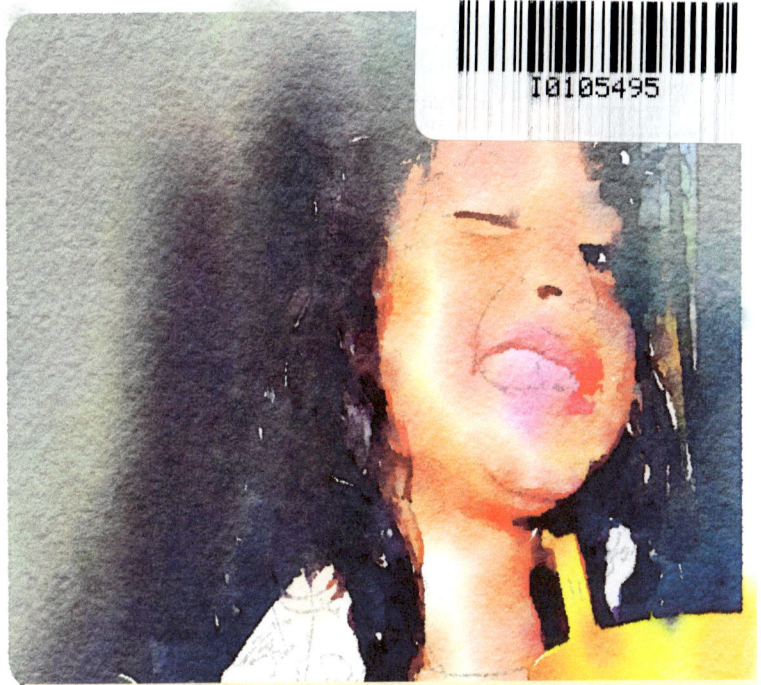

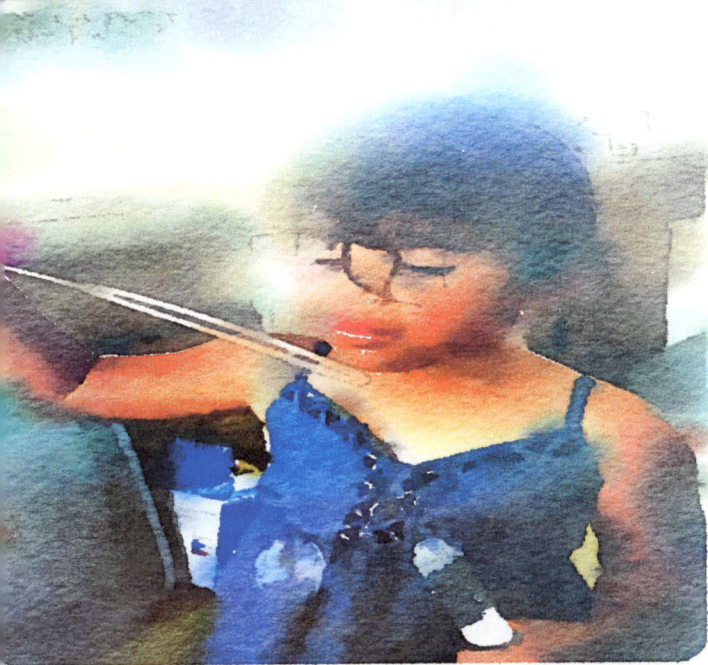

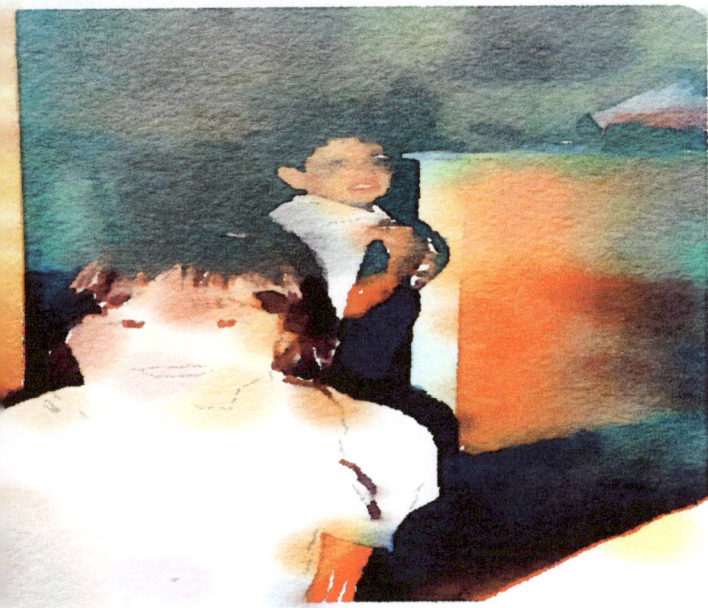

This book is dedicated to my loving
husband Noel who loves all of my ideas and
supports me in all my pursuits. My children
Noel, Gianna, and Noah you are my
shinning stars, dreaming big, and never
give up.
My godchildren Ace, Zaiden and Hailey you
are special aim high.
My niece's Ayrianna, Lauren and Sienna
you are amazing, keep reaching for the
stars and my nephew's Nathan, Isaiah, Eli,
JJ, and Nathaniel you are believing and
achieving greatness.
My little cousins Bree, Celeste and Hailey
you are brilliant and loved.

## With much love

**ISBN-13:978-0692735237**

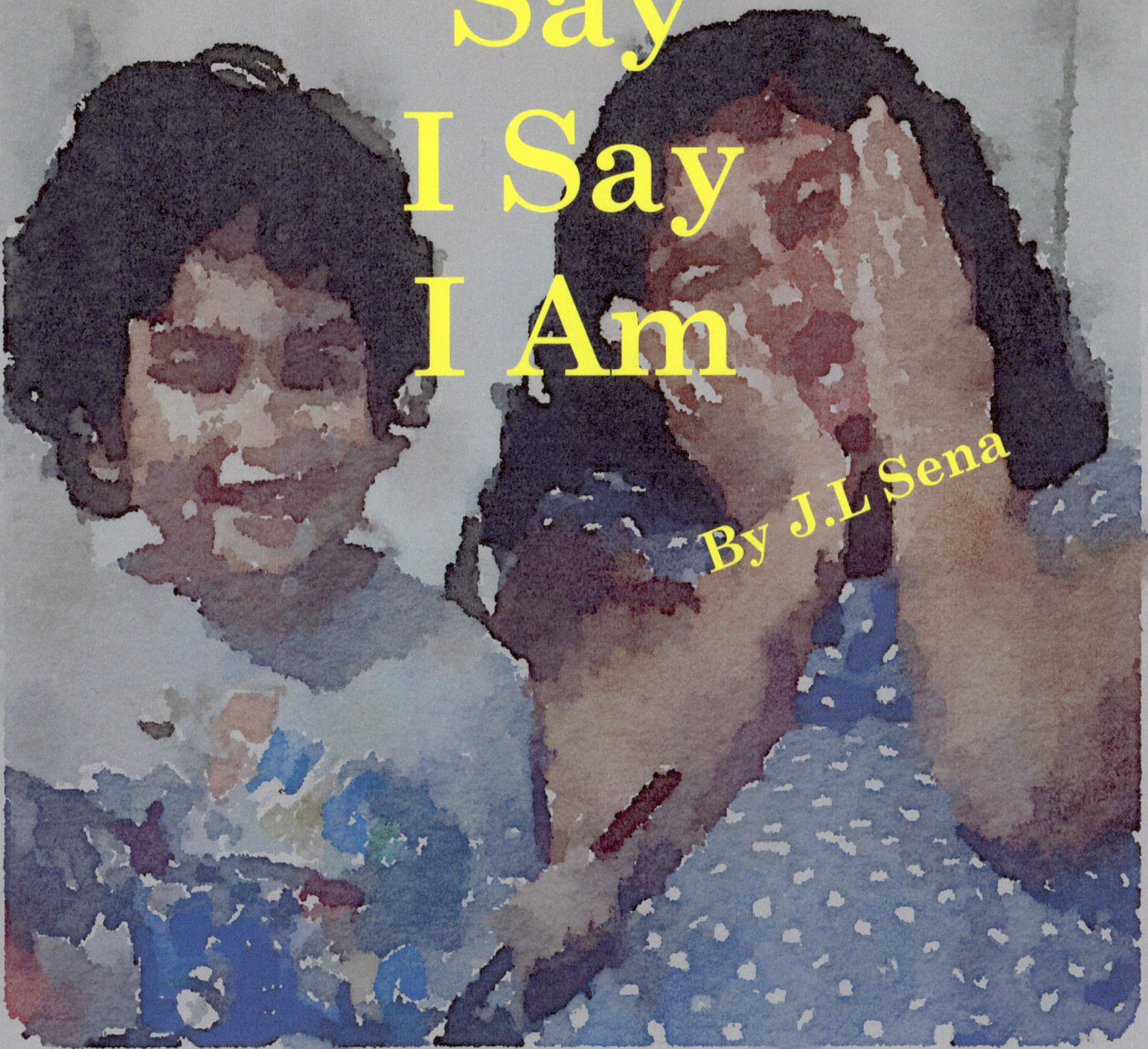

# We
# Say
# I Say
# I Am

By J.L Sena

Mommy said it's always good to say nice things about others and ourselves.

So... We say...

I Am Loved.

I Am Loving.

# I Am Smart.

# I Am Curious.

I Am
Terrific at
learning
something
new
everyday.

I Am a Leader.

Daddy said if we believe in goodness it will be true and we could teach others to do the same too.

So... We say...

I Treat others the way I want
to be Treated.

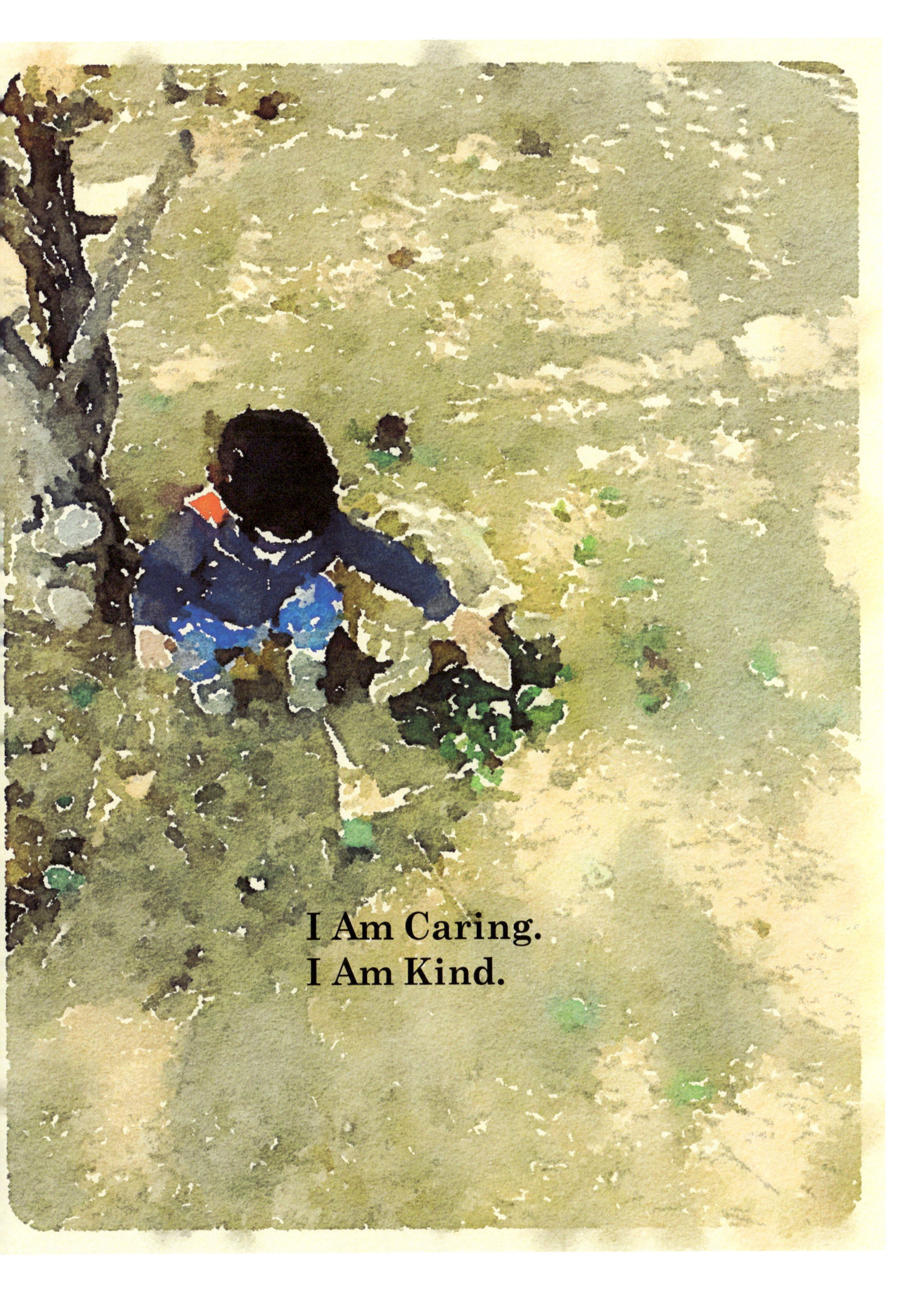

I Am Caring.
I Am Kind.

I Am Powerful.

# I Am a Team Player.

Grandpa and Grandma said if we love ourselves everyone else will too.

So... We say...

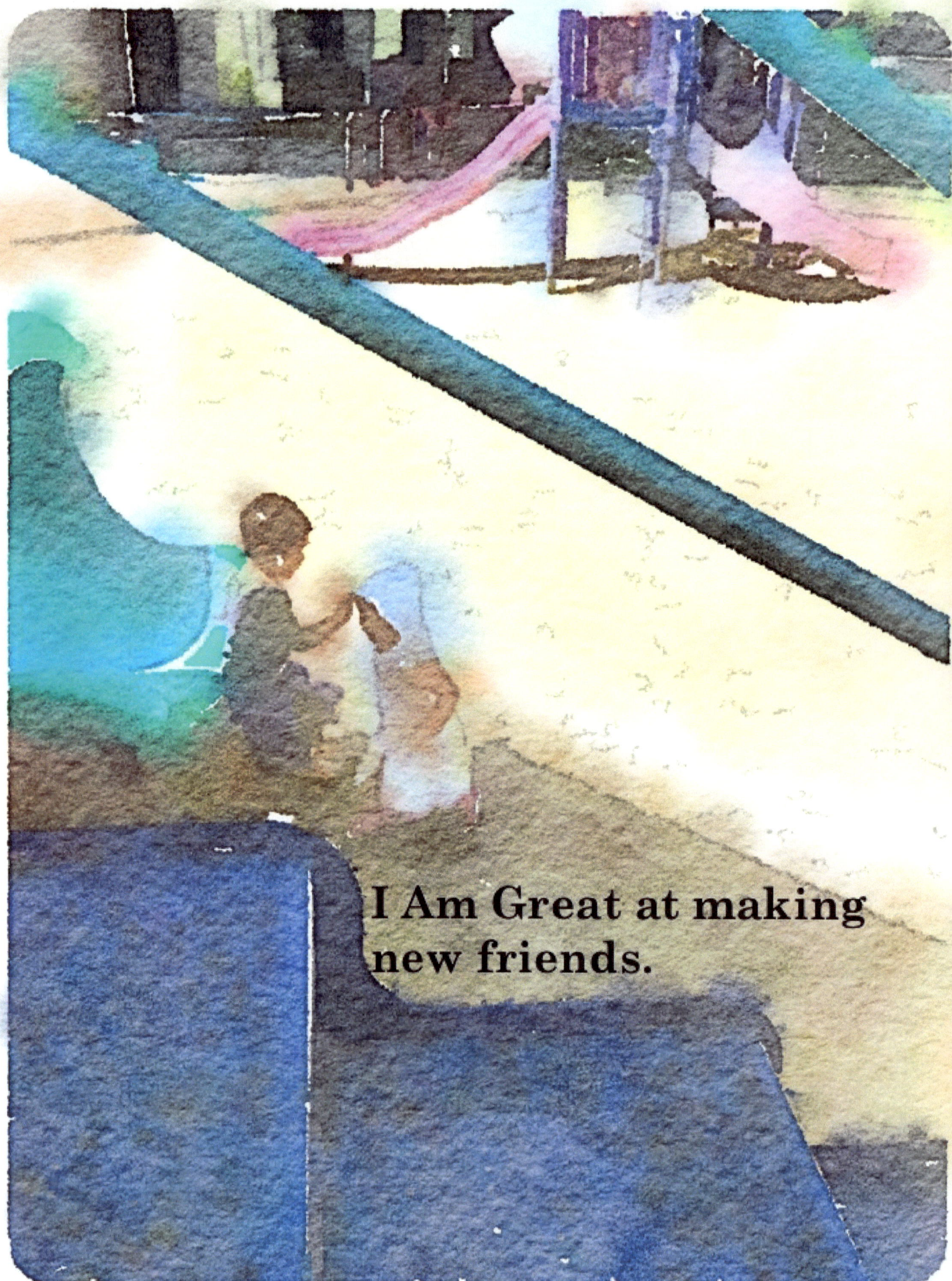

I Am Great at making new friends.

I Believe in myself.

I Am a Champion.

I Can be anything I Believe
I Can be.

Great Grandma said "You are great, but you must say it for it to be true to you".

So... We say...

I Am Great.

I Am Happy.

I Am Strong.

I Am Fantastic.

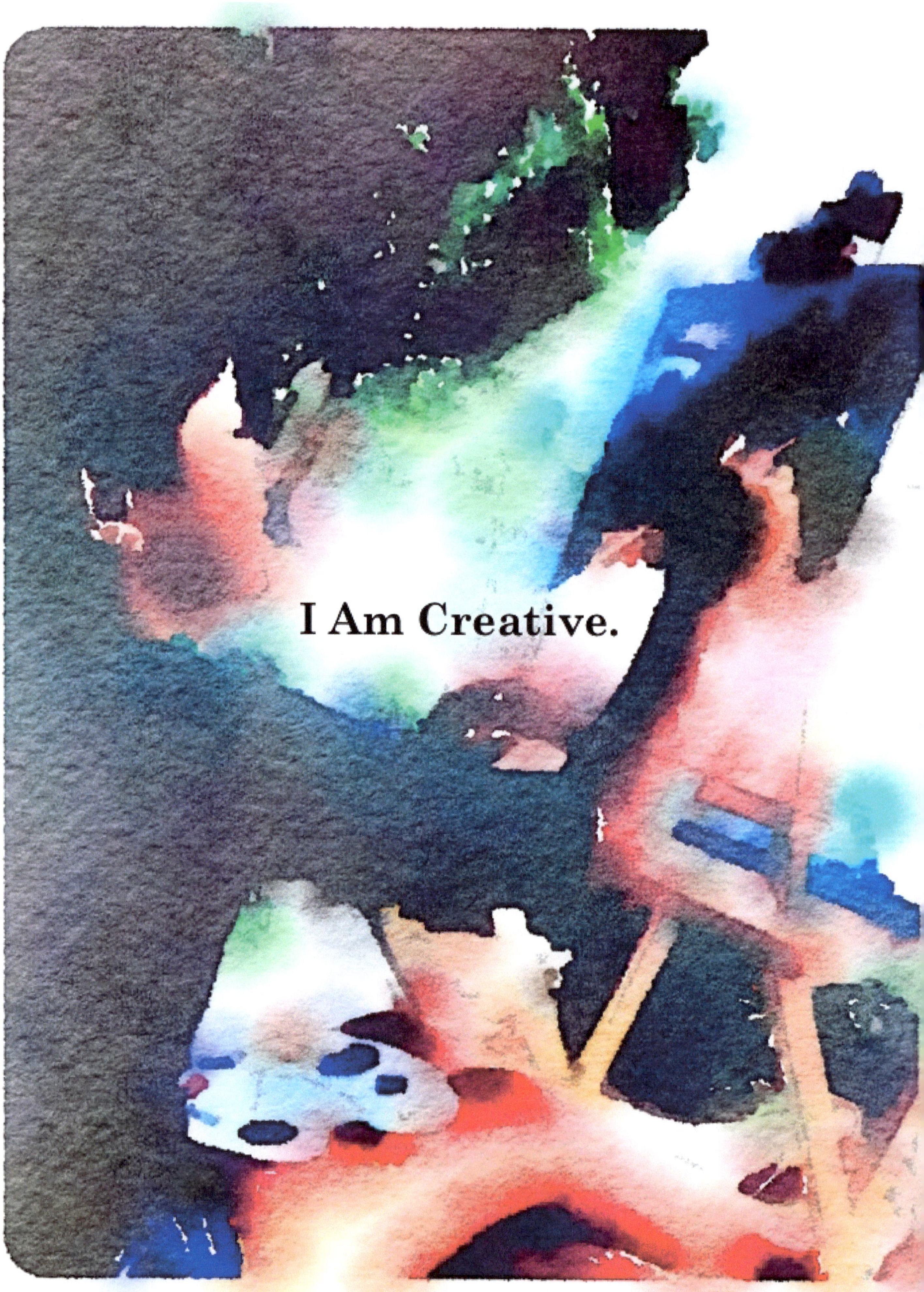
I Am Creative.

I Am Handsome.
I Am Special.

I Am Silly.
I Am Interesting.

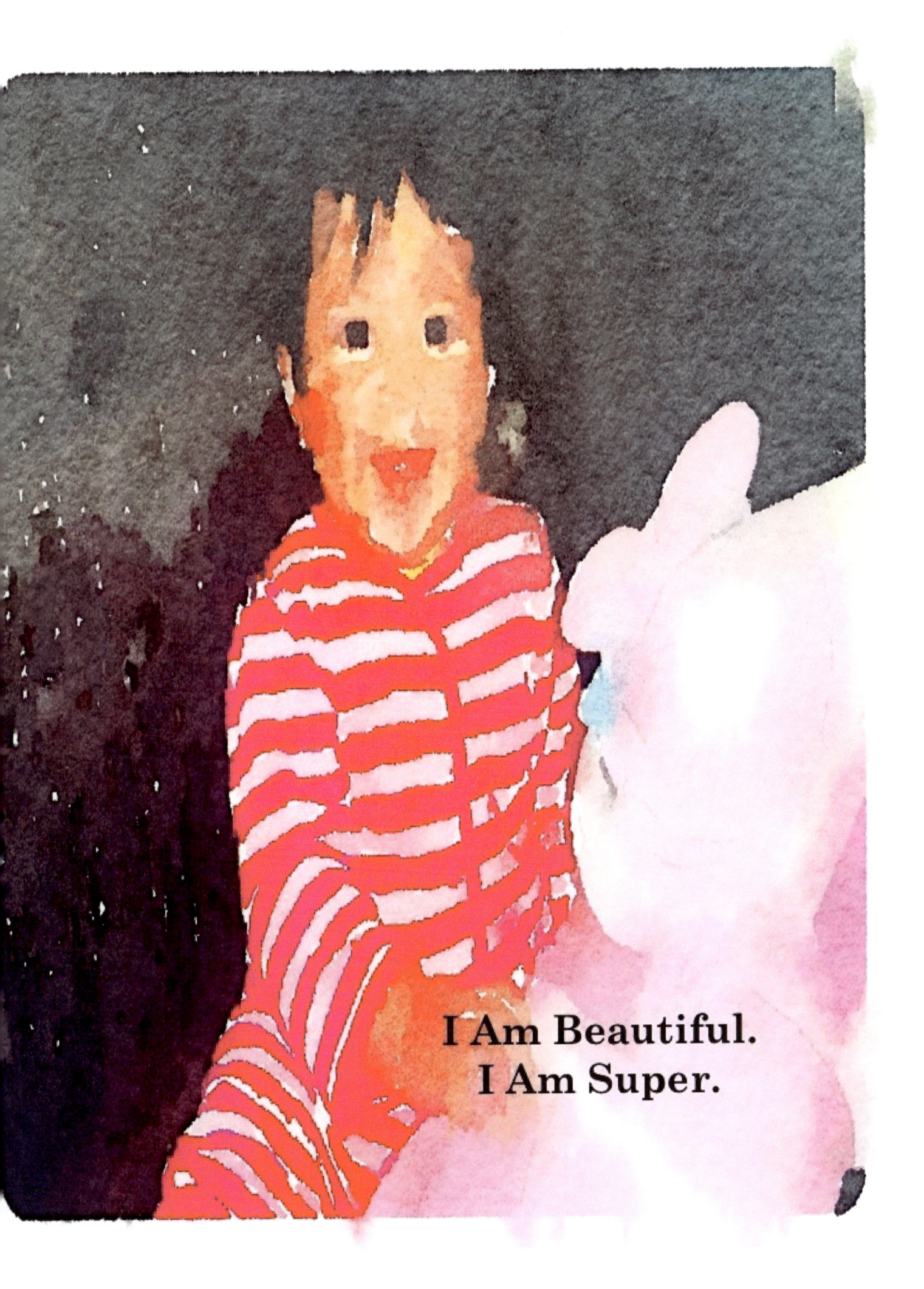

I Am Beautiful.
I Am Super.

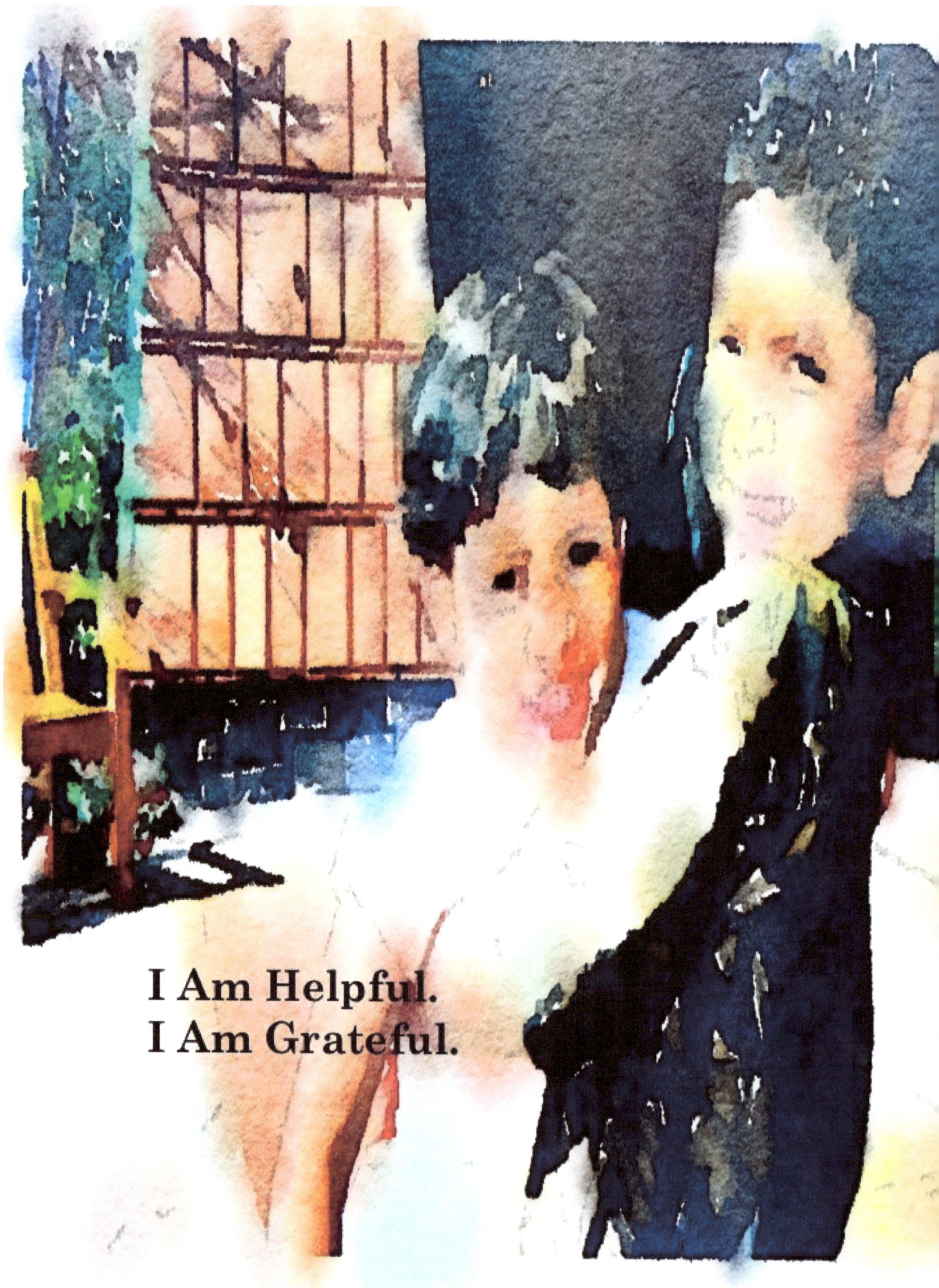

I Am Helpful.
I Am Grateful.

I Am Brave.
I Am Courageous.

I Am Giving.
I Am Cheerful.

# We Say I Say I Am...

Plant a seed
Water it
Nurture it
And
Watch it
Grow and
Bare its
Fruits.

www.ingramcontent.com/pod-product-compliance
Lightning Source LLC
Chambersburg PA
CBHW040231070426
42447CB00030B/101